W9-AWH-157

Gadgets and Gizmos

Thrillogy

Edited by Paul Collins and Meredith Costain

sundance

Read all of the
 Titles

Copyright © 2000 Sundance Publishing

All rights reserved. No part of this publication may be reproduced, stored in a retrieval system or transmitted in any form or by any means, electronic, mechanical, photocopying, recording, or otherwise, without the prior written permission of the publisher.

Published by Sundance Publishing
P.O. Box 1326, 234 Taylor Street, Littleton, MA 01460

Copyright in individual stories remains with the authors.

First published 1999 as Spinouts by
Addison Wesley Longman Australia Pty Limited
95 Coventry Street, South Melbourne 3205 Australia
Exclusive United States Distribution: Sundance Publishing

ISBN 0-7608-4832-7

Printed in Canada

Contents

Headcase

The author
Robert Hood
talks about the story

"The story grew out of strange
thoughts suggested by the word
headcase. It has both a slang meaning (as
in "You're a bit of a headcase, Rob.")
and a more direct meaning. I played
around with the idea and then created
some characters to fit the situation. It
was a lot of fun."

Robert Hood

Headcase

"I scored a neat, new schoolcase," Dirk Pennewick said smugly.

We were waiting at the hover-bus stop. The weather was cold, and I was grumpy.

"It's going to be really popular," Dirk added when he saw that he didn't have my attention. "Everyone will want one."

Dirk's a loser. He's as skinny as a snake on a liquid diet, with a big head that looks like it belongs to someone else. He talks too much, and most of what he says is garbage.

"New schoolcase, eh?" I grumbled. "Big deal."

"It can carry all sorts of stuff." He grinned like a demented hyena. "Dad got it for me." His dad's a hotshot cyberspace architect.

"A hi-tech schoolcase?"

"Sure. Why not? It's the only one of its kind in the world. You want to see it? I've got it right here."

I looked. He wasn't carrying a thing, and there was nothing on the ground near him except a pile of brown muck.

"It looks like dog poo to me," I said, flicking the muck onto his pants with the tip of my shoe. He leaped away like it was going to bite him. I laughed.

"Just for that," he huffed, "I'm not going to show you the case."

"Aw, gee, I'm so sad."

8

The bus arrived before he could think of a reply, so I grabbed my own schoolcase from the far edge of the bench. Dirk slithered up the anti-grav steps, still carrying nothing. So much for the new wonder case! Like most of what Dirk said, it was just a lie.

As I moved past him, I sneered and kept going toward the back of the bus. You can only sit in the back if you're cool, so Dirk had to sit up front. I sit wherever I want. He wasn't happy about it.

I didn't talk to anyone the whole way to school, least of all Dirk. My mind wandered, remembering school back in the good ol' days when you'd wake up in the morning, plug into the VR port next to your bed, enter your ID code, and surf off into cyberschool.

The big turnaround came a few years ago, when everyone started saying that virtual schooling was too antisocial. They said it was creating a generation of selfish cyberbrats. So it was back to real-world schools, where a bunch of teachers bored you to death while you sat in a crowd of smelly idiots, just so you'd learn to get along with other people. Who needs it?

"Watch it, drainhead," I snarled as someone squeezed past me into an empty seat.

The interesting thing was that, when we got to class, Dirk had all of his books and pens. I never saw his schoolcase, but he had whatever he needed the whole day. Somehow he was carrying stuff around: pens, CD-ROMs, books, lunch. He saw me looking and grinned knowingly.

I hate that.

Afterwards, he walked into Tech History empty-handed but still managed to produce an antique, late-twentieth-century laptop computer for Show and Tell. I was ready to give in and become interested.

"Okay," I said in the hall afterward. "Where do you keep your books and pens and stuff?"

"I told you, in my new schoolcase."

"But you're not carrying one."

"Yes, I am."

"Is it invisible?"

"Nope."

"Is it in your pocket?"

"It's not in my pocket, though it's almost small enough."

"Small enough?"

"And did I tell you it can fit tons of stuff in it?"

"Tons of junk!" I growled, fed up with his garbage.

"Whatever." He turned away in a huff.

I grabbed his arm. "Don't get bent out of shape." He gazed up at me, and I noticed there was something weird about his eyes. They looked hollow and cold. I shivered.

"You're never nice to me," he said. "You're always mean."

"Well," I shrugged. "You're pretty low down in the order of things. Somewhere below maggots."

He frowned. "I bet you wouldn't be so cocky if . . ."

"If what?" I poked his skinny chest. "You're not threatening me, are you?"

A smirk slithered over his lips. "I might be."

"Yeah?"

"Yeah."

We went out back, where we could settle this without interruption. Of course, I was a lot bigger than Dirk. He must have known I was going to crush him like a bug. But the unfairness didn't worry me. I never fought fights I couldn't win.

Dirk didn't seem worried, either. He just stood there, staring at me with those cold, empty eyes of his.

"Well?"

"The thing is, Alistair," he said, "my new schoolcase is in here." He tapped the side of his head. "It's a headcase."

"You're a headcase."

"My dad invented it. Special microchips he developed create a virtual space and stuff can be digitally stored in it. Everything's made of electricity, you see, like a pen, for instance. So the headcase breaks the pen down into electrical impulses and stores them inside. When you want to take it out of the headcase again, it re-forms, instantly, from loose atoms in the atmosphere. And it's all controlled by thought. Hey, presto! My pen!"

He held up his hand and a pen appeared in it. It had his name on it.

My mouth dropped open.

"It's a trick!" I exclaimed.

"No trick. My dad decided to try it out on me. It only required a bit of minor surgery . . . a few implants."

"But—"

"Anything I see can be put in the headcase—as long as it isn't larger than, oh, say . . . you!"

His hollow eyes glowed red. A queasy feeling came over me and, for a moment, I felt as though I was coming apart. There was a flash of light, I was flying, and then . . .

Darkness.

The first thing I noticed was that the darkness smelled. I sniffed. It smelled like old apples. I sniffed again. I smelled other things, too, like peanut butter sandwiches and sugary lollipops.

I knew this combination of smells. It's what my

own schoolcase smells like. It's what every kid's schoolcase smells like.

Then I remembered what Dirk had said, and knew I wasn't in a schoolcase. I was in Dirk's headcase!

The thought made me sick. I didn't want to be in Dirk's head—it was probably diseased. I wanted out. Now.

"Let me out of here!" I yelled.

But even as I yelled, I knew I wasn't making a sound. That was because I'd been broken down into electrical impulses and stored digitally in Dirk's head. What a bummer! How could I get out when I was just an electrical impulse?

I reached around in the darkness but couldn't feel anything, not even my own hands.

"Excuse me, but is there someone else in here?"

I could sense a voice, though it sounded strange. And it wasn't my voice.

"Yeah," I said. "I'm in here. Are you in here, too?"

"Yes."

"Who are you?"

"Ellen. Ellen Moore."

Ellen Moore. She was that great-looking girl in Mr. Lee's class. She hadn't been in school the last couple of days. No one knew why.

"What are you doing in here?" I asked.

She snorted angrily.

"I've been stuck here since the day before yesterday. He won't let me out."

"You mean Dirk?"

"Who else? He came up to me and said I was the luckiest girl in the school because he liked me and was willing to hang out with me. I thought he was weird and told him to get lost."

"So he put you in his headcase, huh?"

"Yes. And it smells. I don't like it. What about you?"

I told her about my fight with Dirk, though I made it sound a little less like it was my fault. If Dirk ever let us out of here, I wanted Ellen to think I was a really cool guy.

"Maybe if we yell a lot, someone will hear."

"Okay."

We screamed and shouted. At first nothing happened. I was about to give up, when there was a sudden burst of light. A whole area of darkness above me seemed to open like a lid. A voice boomed around us.

"Shut up!" That was Dirk. I couldn't see him, but I could hear him.

"We're going to keep this up until somebody hears us and makes you let us out!"

"Forget it! No one can hear you. And I don't want to let you out. You were mean to me."

"Maybe I was, but only because you're such a jerk."

It probably wasn't the greatest thing to say. Dirk made an angry sound and the lid of his headcase slammed shut with a thunderous bang.

Time went by. Ellen and I chatted. The stink got worse. Every now and then the lid would open and something would be sucked out with a *whoosh*! Inside the case, nothing had a real shape, so I couldn't tell what was being sucked out. Things came in, too—but unless they could talk, I couldn't tell what they were. It was very annoying.

"Hey, Dirk!" I yelled occasionally. "Let us out!"

"Yeah," Ellen joined in. "I've got better things to do than hang around in here. It's boring."

We might have been stuck in Dirk's headcase forever if it wasn't for Ellen's brilliant idea. She started experimenting with the electrical impulses that were all around us. She discovered that she could create small currents of wind that moved the schoolcase smell around. I joined in, and then every time Dirk opened his headcase, we'd send out gusts of stink.

Dirk didn't notice, of course, because it was his stink—but eventually somebody else noticed.

"Dirk!" boomed an adult voice. "What is that smell?"

"What smell?"

"The smell from your headcase. It's coming out your ears! Have you been putting gross things in there?"

"Nah. Just the normal stuff."

"Well, I think it's time I cleaned it out."

"Aw, no, Dad. It'll be okay."

"No, it won't. I'll take a look with my Impulse Reader. . . ."

"Dirk! There are people in there! Two of them!"

"There are?"

"What did I tell you about putting people in your head?"

Well, Mr. Pennewick got us out, and Dirk was grounded for a month. His headcase was disconnected, and Mr. Pennewick went back to the drawing board with his idea. He plans to put in some safeguards. Our parents called off the police hunt and sued the Pennewicks for damages. Ellen and I hung around together for about a week. But out in the real world, we didn't have much in common and lost interest in one another pretty quickly.

A few days later, Dirk came up to me in the locker room and apologized.

"Forget it!" I said, then shoved him into my locker with three pairs of old gym socks and some dirty underwear.

That'll show him!

The Diplomatic
Hyperspace
Negotiator

The author
Eva Mills
talks about the story

"I came up with the idea of a sort of *virtual reality* where people would be forced to sort out their differences by discussing them calmly and rationally. Then I wondered what would happen if you put a school bully in there. Somehow, I couldn't see things going according to plan."

The Diplomatic Hyperspace Negotiator

The trouble started when Grixel Jackson's Aunt Barla brought back some truth serum from her trip to the Andromeda system.

"I won't drink it! You can't make me!" cried Grixel's victims. Yet Grixel always managed to get the information he needed. It could be the answers to last night's homework, the name of a student who had complained to a teacher, or the best place to buy Galileo Goobers.

Antina Solin was no exception. "You're such a bully, Grixel Jackson!" she cried, struggling as he tied the arms of her space suit together and pinned her to the ground.

Grixel leaned over her and squirted truth serum into her mouth with an eyedropper. "Now," he said. "Tell me where you keep those red beetle-juice cookies your father makes."

"That's Betelgeuse cookies, you nano-ninny," Antina replied through gritted teeth. "Betelgeuse: a red giant star in the Orion sector. They're in my locker, in a plastic container disguised as an electrocyclopedia. They were hidden from you!"

"Not any more!" smirked Grixel, as he turned to raid Antina's lunch.

Antina complained to her parents. "Not only did Grixel steal my Betelgeuse cookies, but before the truth serum wore off, I told Jonas that his space suit looks Plutonian. And he should recycle it. Then I told Tessa that even though she's half android, she should tone down her vocabulary because it gives everyone a headache. And then I told one of the facilitators that he had bad breath."

"But was it all true?" asked Antina's mother, Cairo.

"Of course it was all true. I'd been given truth serum!" wailed Antina. "That's not the point. The point is that Grixel Jackson is a bully, and we have to do something about him."

Antina's father, Jero, sighed. "The learning facility has told us that Grixel's insecurity and lack of parental guidance have led to his poor behavior," he said. "He is receiving maximum counseling support. And they have him on a new, experimental program."

"I can assure you, Antina," said Cairo, "that Grixel's primary caregiver is extremely concerned about his behavior. And that the learning facility is dealing with it in a caring manner."

"Meanwhile, we have to put up with having truth serum poured down our throats," grumbled Antina.

"In your great-great-grandfather's day," said Cairo, "people thought the best way to deal with bullies was to punch them in the nose."

"Terrible," muttered Jero.

"But those barbaric days are long gone," continued Cairo. "Now Earth is a peaceful, nonviolent society. And we have developed much gentler methods of dealing with people who have psychological problems."

Antina sighed. Her parents meant well, but they didn't understand what it was like to have to deal with Grixel's "temporary psychotic episodes" on a daily basis.

Antina expressed her frustrations to her friend, Tessa. "It's getting so bad, Tessa, that I even dream about . . . you know . . . skipping classes and going down to the Entertainment Center."

"Yes," said Tessa grimly. "Things are degenerating rapidly. But see what my sibling Tani gave me last night." Tessa held out a small, black box that fitted into the palm of her hand. There were two small buttons on the smooth surface. "It's a Diplomatic Hyperspace Negotiator," she said.

Antina drew in her breath sharply. "The greatest

invention of the lost race of the Artemisians," she whispered. "Where did she get that?"

"Tani spent a period of time working for an antiques dealer," said Tessa. "This was a sign of his gratitude."

"You mean a thank-you present," said Antina. "But how does it work?"

"Well," began Tessa. "As you know, the Artemisians were a gentle people. They were known for their ability to resolve all disputes through discussion and mediation, without violence."

"Yeah," said Antina. "Unlike Grixel Jackson."

"Exactly," said Tessa, her eyes blazing. "Once I press these two buttons and direct the laser beam at Grixel Jackson, he and I will be transported into the Diplomatic Hyperspace. Then the Virtual Mediator will assist us in resolving our differences. I am sure that Grixel will be persuaded to see the error of his ways."

"Slow down a minute," said Antina. "You mean you both go into the Hyperspace. You talk to Grixel about what's wrong with his behavior. And he has to listen?"

"Correct," nodded Tessa.

"I've got to see this!" said Antina.

"That will not be possible," said Tessa. "While Grixel and I are in the Diplomatic Hyperspace, we shall appear frozen in time to any observers."

"I'm sure you know what you're doing," said Antina, eyeing the black box nervously. "Now we just have to wait for Grixel to choose today's victim."

"Grixel's after me!" yelled Jonas Lansing. He sprinted down the hall toward Tessa and Antina. "Run for your lives!"

Tessa stepped into the hallway facing Grixel as he

raced after Jonas. She held the Negotiator in front
of her like a shield. "Stop right there, Grixel
Jackson," she said. "Or I shall have no choice but
to zap you with the Diplomatic Hyperspace
Negotiator."

"Ha!" laughed Grixel scornfully. "Get out of my way, you piece of jabbering space junk. You couldn't zap me with a seven-yard superconductor even if you tried."

So, Tessa zapped him.

"What happened?" asked Jonas, as he waved his hands in front of Grixel's unseeing eyes. Tessa, too, was frozen to the spot, arm extended with the Negotiator in her hand.

"They're in the Diplomatic Hyperspace," explained Antina. "The Virtual Mediator is helping them to resolve their differences. There's nothing we can do but wait."

So they waited. And waited. And waited.

"Aarrgghh!" Grixel reeled back with a cry, his hands to his face. Blood was pouring through his fingers.

"Grixel!" cried Jonas. "Are you okay?"

"Get me away from her," cried Grixel, eyeing Tessa nervously. "Now!"

Jonas led Grixel in the direction of the Medication Room. Antina turned to face Tessa. She still had a dazed expression on her face.

"What happened?" asked Antina. "Tell me what happened!"

"Well . . . " said Tessa, slowly. "We entered the Diplomatic Hyperspace and found ourselves in a large, open room."

"Did you see the Virtual Mediator?" asked Antina.

"Yes," said Tessa, frowning. "It was more of a presence than a person. It seemed to reflect my features first and then Grixel's. It was almost as if it were using our reflections to generate its own images of us."

"Did it tell Grixel to stop being such a bully?"

"Not really," said Tessa. "The Virtual Mediator asked us to discuss our differences calmly and rationally. I expressed my opinion that Grixel is a cruel bully. And that he picks on his fellow students just because he likes the feeling of being able to dominate others. Grixel told me I was an overblown gas bag and that my parents should have left me on Hyperion Two when they had the chance. I suggested that it would be preferable if Grixel stopped his antisocial behavior. Grixel suggested that it would be preferable if everyone took a supersonic jump into a Venusian swamp."

Antina's mouth dropped. "And then what happened?" she asked.

"Well, then the Virtual Mediator asked Grixel to try and express his opinions logically and objectively. So Grixel turned to the Virtual Mediator and said, 'You're a stupid piece of outdated techno-trash. You can take my opinions and shove them down your garbage disposal. And then you can go and get your molecules rearranged.'"

"He said that?" gasped Antina. "But what happened next?"

"Then the Virtual Mediator punched Grixel in the nose," said Tessa. "And that concluded the Diplomatic Hyperspace Negotiation."

Some time later, Antina's parents asked her whether Grixel's behavior had improved. She was able to report a satisfying improvement in his social interaction.

"Grixel's fine now," said Antina. "He hasn't bullied anyone for months. And he's doing his best to be nice to everyone. Particularly Tessa," she added.

"It seems like the counseling Grixel received at the learning facility did wonders for him," said Cairo.

"Whatever they tried on him was obviously very effective," said Jero.

"Oh, I'd say the treatment was effective, all right," said Antina with a small smile. "*Very* effective."

Room
for
Improvement

The author
Michael Pryor
talks about the story

"I've always liked writing about characters who are quick on their feet. But then I started wondering about someone like that whose mouth tended to run away with him or her and the trouble that could get him or her in."

Michael Pryor

Room for Improvement

Sarah sighed, as she skated down the hill toward home. Her schoolbag bumped against her back, and she thought she could hear the pieces of her calculator rattling around inside.

"Mom will kill me," she muttered, and coasted around the corner. She neatly avoided the streetlight and powered up the sidewalk. "But it wasn't my fault."

The first part wasn't true; the second part was. The broken calculator wasn't her fault. It was Mandy Grundig's fault.

Lots of things were Mandy Grundig's fault. All of the kids knew that. Squashed bananas in your schoolbag, broken rulers, missing pencils, those kinds of things were The Grunter's fault. And she did all of them with that mean smile that said: "You think that's bad? Just you wait."

And of course, The Grunter was huge. She loved lifting weights. She also liked dropping them on people.

The trouble was, The Grunter was plain mean. Sarah had tried being nice, tried ignoring her, tried everything. But still she suffered from The Grunter's behavior, like everyone else.

The calculator was the latest catastrophe, and all because Sarah had been daydreaming during math. "What are you looking at?" Mandy had hissed. Sarah realized that she'd been looking in The Grunter's direction. And before Sarah could stop them, the words popped out of her mouth. "I think it's a giant slug, but I'm not sure."

As soon as she said it, Sarah knew she was doomed. But she never could stop her mouth. Sometimes it just had a life of its own. She put her head in her hands.

When the class finished, The Grunter stomped past Sarah's desk and knocked her calculator onto the floor.

Then she crushed it with her foot. "I'm sorry," The Grunter said sarcastically, then waddled off.

The memory made Sarah's stomach flip-flop, and she stopped for a moment outside the stores.

She saw that a new store had opened, in between the old picture framer's shop and the abandoned

pet store. "FIXIT" it said in large letters, and underneath in smaller letters: "We Repair Anything!"

Sarah didn't stop to think. She skated right in.

Inside the small shop, Sarah saw rows of shelves. On them were toasters, tennis rackets, fish tanks, watches, radios, shoes, birdcages, and sewing machines. And all of them had parts missing or were broken.

Behind the counter was a tall, thin woman, with hair the color of a cloudy sky. "I'm Ms. Fixit. What can I do for you?" she said, over her glasses.

"Can you fix calculators?" Sarah asked.

"The sign outside says 'Anything'," the woman said. "Let me see it."

Sarah handed over the mangled calculator, and the woman peered at it closely. "Five minutes," she announced, and disappeared through a curtained doorway.

She was back in two. "One dollar, please."

"Will it work?" Sarah asked doubtfully.

"Better than ever," the woman said. Then she smiled. "Or your money back."

It was when Sarah was doing her homework that she noticed there was something strange going on with the calculator.

She could talk to it.

Sarah found this out because she always read math problems out loud. And after she read the first one, the numbers appeared on the calculator's tiny screen.

Sarah's eyes opened wide, and after she experimented a little, she believed it. She suddenly had a voice-activated calculator!

All of the next day at school, Sarah thought about her calculator. Ms. Fixit had really fixed it. In fact, it was better than ever.

Even The Grunter's efforts didn't distract Sarah.

"Watch it, pimple," Mandy growled in the hallway, and elbowed Sarah in the back.

"I don't have to watch it, I can smell it," Sarah's mouth said, and The Grunter's face turned purple.

Sarah was saved by the principal, who happened to be walking by. Sarah scampered out the door before The Grunter could mangle her.

Sarah raced home as fast as her in-line skates would take her. In the back of her closet, she found her old clock radio, the one that had stopped working when she'd accidentally dropped it in the fish tank.

"Not a problem," Ms. Fixit declared when Sarah took it in the next day. "Soon it'll be better than ever."

"I'm looking forward to this," Sarah said when the spindly woman trotted back and accepted the dollar Sarah gave her.

Sarah had never been able to find an alarm that worked for her. She could stay asleep with a steam roller crushing a dozen pianos next to her. So that night, she set the alarm eagerly.

She woke up to an earthquake.

The bed was shaking, her teeth were rattling, and she felt like she was inside a washing machine.

With a thud, she fell out of bed. "Good," a voice said. "It's about time."

Even though she was sitting on the cold floor with only her pajamas on, Sarah giggled. The voice had come from her improved clock radio. When she examined it, she found a small dial set into the base. She was sure it hadn't been there before. The dial had settings marked "Earthquake," "Thunderstorm," "Hail," and "Lightning."

She shuddered and gently put down the machine. There was no way she wanted to be fried by a lightning bolt in bed!

As she skated to school, Sarah thought hard. The improvements to her calculator and clock radio were amazing. "Magical," she said to herself, as she skillfully avoided a garbage can on the sidewalk.

That was when she sped around a blind corner and ran into The Grunter.

As Sarah bounced off her and sailed through the air, she found herself thinking that she had a serious problem.

She landed painfully on her shoulder, then slid along the sidewalk on her back. Her schoolbag felt as if it was filled with barbed wire.

When she opened her eyes, she saw The Grunter standing over her. She was so big she blocked out the sun.

"You!" The Grunter snarled, looking as if her muscles were about to explode. "You again!"

42

Sarah scrambled to her feet, barely avoiding The Grunter's massive arms.

"Come back here!" The Grunter roared as Sarah ducked. "Your time is up!"

"Really? What number is the big hand on?"

"You're history!"

"Has anyone ever told you that you have a face like a pizza pie? With pepperoni?"

Sarah glided backward as The Grunter stumbled after her. She could hardly believe what her own mouth was saying. She thought with dismay, did I really call The Grunter a pizza face? I should wear a gag.

Then Sarah noticed that The Grunter was wearing

in-line skates. They looked like baby boots on an elephant, because her feet were the only tiny thing about her. Sarah knew that they were the same size as her feet, because The Grunter had borrowed Sarah's sneakers one day in gym class, without asking, of course.

But as Sarah easily avoided The Grunter's reach, she noticed that her enemy was just a clumsy beginner. "I'd love to stop and chat," Sarah grinned, "but there are people I can do that with."

The screech that followed Sarah down the street was enough to break glass. I've done it again, Sarah thought. Why can't I keep my big mouth shut?

When school finished, Sarah grabbed her skates. A note fluttered out as they fell to pieces. "Let's see how well you can skate with these, Motor Mouth."

Sarah didn't have to see a signature to know it was the work of The Grunter. She frowned and said, "Another job for Ms. Fixit," and sprinted down the road.

"Ah, Sarah," said Ms. Fixit. "I knew you'd be back."

"Here," Sarah panted. "My in-line skates. Broken."

Ms. Fixit waved her hand. "I know that, I know that. But I fix more important things than appliances and equipment, you know."

"You do?" Sarah asked.

"Problems, for instance. I fix problems."

Sarah stared at the gray-haired woman. "How?" she asked.

Ms. Fixit raised an eyebrow. "Now, that's the thing. You won't know how until it's fixed. Do you have any problems, Sarah?"

Sarah thought about a problem she had. A problem the size of a mountain. And twice as mean.

"Yes," she said firmly. "But I just want my skates fixed, thank-you. I can handle my problems myself."

"Now, that's what I like to hear. As soon as you say that, your problem's half-solved." She chuckled again. "Of course, a little help never hurts." And whistling, she disappeared into her back room.

When Ms. Fixit came back, she had two small robots in her hands.

At least, they looked like robots. After staring for a moment, Sarah recognized them as her in-line skates.

They were covered with bright chrome and had gears and levers sticking out at all angles.

"Now they're better than ever. One dollar, please."

In a daze, Sarah paid and stumbled out of the shop. She stood blinking in the sunlight, holding her new and improved skates as if they might blast off at any moment.

"Thanks. I'll just take those." The voice was snarly, mean, and it belonged to The Grunter.

"Hey!" Sarah cried. "They're mine!"

"Well, I'll just borrow them for a while. Say, five or six years," The Grunter smirked.

Sarah watched helplessly as The Grunter strapped the skates on her brawny legs. "I don't think you should do that," she began, but The Grunter cut her off.

"Too late!" she crowed, and stood up, arms waving to keep her balance.

The burst of light took Sarah by surprise. It erupted from the back of the skates, and an earsplitting scream followed.

Then, with smoke pouring from the skates, The Grunter started rolling faster and faster up the hill.

Her pace increased rapidly until, just before the top of the hill, she was a blur of speed.

When she reached the top, she took off.

Sarah watched as The Grunter's smoke trail stretched across the sky. Soon, she'd lost sight of the tiny dot her enemy had become.

"Problem solved," Sarah said, and heard a soft, popping noise from behind her. When she turned, the magical repair shop had disappeared.

Sarah shrugged and looked at the sky again. "Yes, it's a major improvement."

About the Illustrators

The Story Illustrator
Terry Denton

Terry Denton was born in another time, on another planet in a far-off galaxy. He came to Earth as an android with a bonus writing chip and an upgraded zip-drive right arm for greater drawing capability. When he is not writing or illustrating, he sits in a dark cabinet with his batteries turned off. "I loved drawing for **Thrillogy** because I love reading science fiction. I decided to do them in a comic-strip style . . . because I also love comics. Drawing in black line only, is always a challenge."

The Cover Illustrator
Marc McBride

Marc McBride has illustrated covers for several magazines and children's books. Marc currently creates the realistic images for his covers using acrylic ink with an airbrush. To solve his messy studio problem, he plans to use computer graphics instead.